MITTENS TO KNIT

20 Contemporary Styles for Men, Women and Children

Mary Lamb Becker

Dover Publications, Inc., New York

Look for these symbols as a guide to patterns for beginning, intermediate and advanced knitters.

Pattern Abbreviations

k — knit
p — purl
oz — ounce(s)
dec — decrease, decreasing
inc — increase, increasing
beg — beginning
st(s) — stitch(es)
ss — stockinette stitch: on 2 needles, alternate rows of k and p; on 4 needles, k every round
sl — slip
tog — together
rep — repeat, repeating
in(s) — inch(es)
Rnd — round
ssk — slip the first stitch as if to knit, slip the second stitch as if to knit, insert the left needle in the fronts of these two stitches from the left and knit

Photography: Mike Huibregtse
Illustrations: Jan Kumbier

Copyright © 1978, 1983 by Mary Lamb Becker.
All rights reserved under Pan American and International Copyright Conventions.

Published in Canada by General Publishing Company, Ltd., 30 Lesmill Road, Don Mills, Toronto, Ontario.

Published in the United Kingdom by Constable and Company, Ltd., 10 Orange Street, London WC2H 7EG.

This Dover edition, first published in 1983, is a new selection of material from the work first published in 1978 by Reiman Publications, Inc., Milwaukee, Wisconsin, under the title *The Mitten Book*.

Manufactured in the United States of America
Dover Publications, Inc., 31 East 2nd Street, Mineola, N.Y. 11501

Library of Congress Cataloging in Publication Data

Becker, Mary Lamb.
  Mittens to knit.

  (Dover needlework series)
  "A new selection of material from the work first published in 1978 by Reiman Publications, Inc., Milwaukee, Wisconsin, under the title The mitten book"—Verso t.p.
  1. Knitting. 2. Gloves. I. Title. II. Series.
TT825.B3825   1983   746.9'2   83-7193
ISBN 0-486-24577-2

TIPS FOR KNITTING MITTENS

Bundle up chilly hands with any of these easy-to-knit patterns that can be worn plain or with worked-on designs by infants, teens and adults.

Beginner? Advanced? What do I knit?
Although a subjective evaluation, the mitten patterns in this book have been graded according to difficulty. Beginners who know how to knit, purl, increase and decrease on straight needles should be able to work beginner patterns with ease. Intermediate knitters should know the difference between a decrease that slants right or left, be able to handle four needle knitting and know how to change colors without leaving holes. Advanced knitters are those who can handle the most difficult patterns on either two or four needles.

What size mitten do I knit?
All the patterns in this book are given in sizes of so many inches. This is *not* comparable to a commercial size glove or mitten, but rather is the actual size of the mitten itself, measured just above the thumb.

To select the correct size, take a tape measure and lap it to the size indicated on the pattern. Slip this over the hand and you will see exactly how much "wiggle room" your wearer's fingers will have. Remember in selecting a size, a closely fitted mitten will not be as warm as one that is slightly loose.

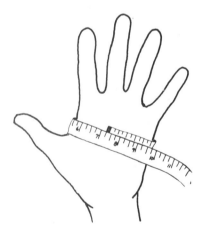

Why you won't see needle sizes in this book
Most patterns suggest a needle size and then add ". . . or the size required to reach gauge."

What confuses most knitters is that the size recommended in no way guarantees that the knitter will reach the proper gauge; it is simply the size used by the average knitter—whoever that is.

A better method is to make a sample swatch. If the suggested gauge is five stitches to the inch, take the yarn you plan to use and cast on 25 sts. Work in stockinette stitch for several inches, starting with a size 8 needle.

Do you get too few stitches per inch? Then switch to a smaller size needle and try again. Too many stitches per inch? Try a larger size. *The gauge is what's important*—not the needle size.

Some people grip metal needles much tighter and knit more tightly than with plastic. The way *you* hold the needle, how you trail the yarn through your fingers, your emotional state (are you tired or tense?) and your physical condition determine the result—your gauge.

Even different colors of knitting worsted can change your gauge, so take the time to try a swatch before each project. The result will be an exact size mitten.

How to get a perfect fit
If you're going to put your time and love into making a pair of mittens, why not have them fit well? The best way is to try on the mitten at various stages of development. But there are a few ways to make this easier.

First of all, divide the stitches of a two needle mitten on at least three needles (more would be better) so the mitten can be drawn around the hand as it will be when the seam is sewed. You could also use a circular needle.

For an infant, where there is the danger of accidentally poking the baby with a needle, try slipping the mitten to a piece of yarn. There are problems with this method, however, such as stitches "letting go" and stretching out of shape at the upper edge, or the hassle of getting your work back on to the needles.

Except for a few cases with size-limiting designs, the patterns in this book say "work even until you reach the angle of the thumb and index finger." Follow the **X** on the diagram as a reference point for controlling the depth of the thumb gore or fixing the position of the thumb opening. It is very important for a good fit.

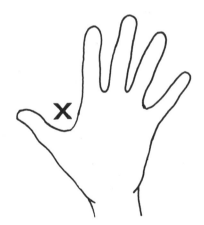

Tape measure or ruler?
Use a tape measure *only* to get the right size mitten. Use a ruler to check gauge.

Keeping track of your stitches
The number of stitches in a row or round after an increase or decrease has been worked are indicated in this book by a number in parentheses—(43). This number represents the stitches *after* the increase or decrease has been worked.

Another use of parentheses you'll find is to simplify

directions like k 3, p 2, k 1, p 1, k 1, p 1—simplified it would read "k 3, p 2, (k 1, p 1) twice."

How to read the charts
All the charts in this book should be read from the bottom up. Odd-numbered rows are read from right to left and even-numbered rows are read from left to right.

Casting on too tight?
If you can't seem to loosen up your cast-on stitches, try casting on with a larger size needle, or even two needles held together.

Perfect hems
Styles with hems are formed by working a purl row on the right side of the stockinette stitch. This allows you to fold the mitten on that line and have a sharp crease.

Super stretchy cuffs
If you like more "give" and stretch in your cuffs, knit into the back loop of each knit stitch. This will twist the stitch and give the ribbing a nice irregularity.

Give stitches a tug
When removing stitches from a holder that is smaller than the needle, give each stitch a tug when you get it onto the needle. This will restore it to original size.

Picking up a stitch
To pick up a stitch, simply draw a loop of yarn through the edge of the knitting with your needle. If you find this awkward, use a fine crochet hook to pull the loop through, then slip it to your needle.

A trick for loose stitches
Here's a tip for four needle knitting: If you notice loose stitches at the ends of the needles, you may want to slip the first stitch of each needle to the next needle on the right after it has been knit. This, in effect, moves that loose area one stitch to the left on each round and makes it less noticeable.

Twisting colors of yarn
In using more than one color of yarn, adjoining colors must be twisted together to avoid holes in your knitting. Drop the color you've just used over the color to be picked up. This will automatically twist them. In a pattern such as Scandinavian Valentine on page 13, where colors are carried over several stitches, yarn should be twisted periodically to prevent long "floaters" on the inside of the mitten.

Weaving in yarn ends like a pro
Thread yarn end into blunt pointed needle and weave through the backs of a few stitches in one direction. Then weave through the backs of a few stitches in the opposite direction, taking care not to allow weaving to show on right side—for a much neater, finished look.

Leave a tail
When cutting off yarn after weaving in the end, allow a "tail" of ⅜ to ½ inch. This is less likely to pop through to the right side than a shorter stub.

One at a time
When using a double strand of yarn and weaving in the ends, weave one strand at a time for a nicer finish.

Thumb too airy?
If the last row of stitches in the tip of your mitten's thumb is too loose, try weaving over and under and around the tip once or twice to fill in. It solves the problem and looks neat too!

Mend those holes
Holes around the base of your mitten's thumb? There's nothing wrong with mending until you find what you're doing to cause holes. But mend lightly. Pulling stitches together makes more holes. Use the duplicate stitch. It's not only permissible, it's inventive!

Weaving the fingertip
Divide the stitches evenly on two double pointed needles, or on single pointed needles. Keep points toward the right. Yarn should be coming from the last stitch on the right of the back needle. If not, thread the yarn into a blunt pointed needle and attach it at that point.

If yarn is attached to the right end of front needle, pass yarn through loop below first stitch on right side of back needle (from top to bottom on the wrong side).

When yarn is correctly positioned, start to weave. Draw yarn through first stitch on front needle *purlwise*, leaving stitch on needle. *Draw yarn through next stitch on back needle *knitwise*, leaving stitch on needle. Draw yarn through same stitch on front needle *knitwise*, slipping stitch off needle. Draw yarn through next stitch on front needle *purlwise*, leaving stitch on needle. Draw yarn through same stitch on back needle *purlwise*, slipping stitch off. Repeat from * until one stitch remains on each needle. Then draw yarn *knitwise* through stitch on front needle and slip stitch off needle. Draw yarn *purlwise* through stitch on back needle and slip off. Weave in end on inside.

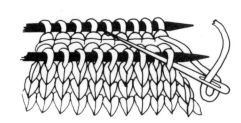

Make a simple stitch marker
Commercial plastic stitch markers (shaped like little lifesavers) are inexpensive and convenient to use in most two needle knitting work. When using four needles, however, where the space between needles needs to be marked, these plastic markers would fall off.

To solve that problem, make a thread marker. You'll need about 12 inches of very fine crochet cotton or similar thread. (If you use yarn, it may cause a slight distortion in the knitting.)

Tie the ends in an overhand knot and weave the looped end up through one or two rows between the last stitch on the right hand needle and the next stitch on the left hand needle.

Thereafter, slip the loop from the left to right needle working yarn alternately in front of and behind the loop (if you are working on four needles).

If you're using single pointed needles, always pass the working yarn behind the loop. The loop will automatically be woven in and out as you work back and forth. When the loop has been drawn its entire length through the work, cut off knot and it will continue to slip up as work progresses.

Bobbin bounty

Find yourself on a weekend without enough bobbins and there's no store open? A styrofoam meat or produce tray can be cut up into pieces about 3 by 6 inches. With a groove cut in at each end to keep yarn from sliding off and a slit on the side, these trays make excellent emergency replacements for commercial bobbins.

Weighing yarns

A postal scale, sold at most U.S. post offices, can be used quite effectively to weigh small amounts of yarn.

"Mitten keeps"

One way to keep mittens from getting lost or misplaced by children is to make a "mitten keep"—a cord that's slipped through the jacket sleeves and sewn to each mitten.

Twisted cord

4 yards of yarn make 27 inches of cord. Slip yarn through electric beater, hold the two ends together and turn mixer on low speed. Hold yarn taut.

Or, loop yarn through a drawer handle and tie the ends to a pencil. Twist by hand, holding the yarn rather taut. When yarn is twisted tightly, grasp it in the middle and cut the loop holding it to the beater or drawer handle. Hold all four ends together and let go of the middle. Allow both halves of the cord to twist together by themselves.

To join two colors of cord, twist 4 yards of the first color and set aside, then twist 4 yards of the second color. Slip the end you are holding through the looped end of the first twisted cord and slide the first cord to the middle of the second cord. Cut the loop of the second cord and hold the ends together, allowing the second cord to twist around the first.

Finger looped cord

Cut a single strand of yarn, 6 times as long as the finished cord length you want. Make a slip knot at the midpoint and slip the loop on your left finger. *Note:* Pulling one end of the yarn will tighten the slip knot, and pulling the other end of the yarn will tighten the loop on your finger.

Reach your right finger through the loop and hook the yarn that tightens the knot. Pull it through the loop and let the original loop slip off your left finger. (You now have another loop on your right finger.) Pull the other end of the yarn, tightening the first loop.

Reach your left finger through the new loop on your right finger. Hook the yarn that tightened the last loop and pull it through the loop on your finger, letting the second loop slip off your finger. Pull the opposite end of the yarn to tighten the second loop.

Continue to pull loops from opposite ends of the yarn, tightening each loop with the same amount of tension each time. To lock the cord, cut both ends of yarn and pull a final loop on your finger until an end slips through the previous loop. Pull both ends tightly.

Made with a single strand of yarn, this cord is fine enough for a mitten cuff tie. If worked double strand, an even more durable cord is made.

Spool knitting cord

You can buy a knitting knobby or make one with a wooden spool and some short finishing nails (without heads). Pound 4 nails as close to the center hole as possible, allowing the nails to stick up about $3/8$ inch. The opening should be at least $3/8$ inch in diameter.

Thread your "knitting knobby" by dropping the end of the yarn through the center hole, allowing it to extend several inches from the bottom. Wind the yarn around the four posts or nails as illustrated. To knit, wind the yarn around the outside of the first post. Holding the yarn firmly against the post, lift the first loop (on the bottom) up over the yarn you are holding, using a short knitting needle. This forms another loop.

Repeat this in a clockwise direction around the spool, tugging at the end of the yarn after each "stitch." To finish, thread the yarn through a blunt needle and draw the yarn through each of the 4 loops. Pull tight.

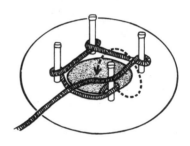

So cute and so warm for tiny little hands...

Baby Rib

There's no time like the present to dress up your favorite little doll in this adorable ribbed and tied mitten. This mitten is just right for keeping baby's hands toasty!

Size: 5 inches.
Yarn: 1 oz Sportweight.
Needles: 1 set double point in size needed to reach gauge.
Gauge: In stockinette stitch, 6 stitches (sts) per inch.

RIGHT MITTEN

Cuff: Cast on 33 sts. Divide on 3 needles being careful not to twist. Work in rib of k 1, p 2 for 1¾ ins.

Beading Rounds: (K 1, p 2 tog, yo) 11 times.
Next Rnd: (K 1, p 1, p yo) 11 times.
Resume rib pattern, working even for 1 in.

Thumb Opening: With contrasting yarn, k 5 sts. Sl these 5 sts back to left needle and k them again with mitten yarn. Work rib pattern to end of Rnd.

Finish Hand: Continue working in rib pattern until mitten is ¾ in less than desired finished length.

Decrease for Tip:
Rnd 1: P 2 tog, p 12, (p 2 tog) twice, p 13, p 2 tog (29).
Rnd 2: P 2 tog, p 10, (p 2 tog) twice, p 11, p 2 tog (25).
Rnd 3: P 2 tog, p 8, (p 2 tog) twice, p 9, p 2 tog (21).
Rnd 4: P 2 tog, p 6, (p 2 tog) twice, p 7, p 2 tog (17).
Rnds 5 and 6: P 2 tog around, ending with p 1 (9, 5). Draw yarn through remaining 5 sts, pull tight and fasten.

Thumb: Each Rnd of thumb is p. Remove contrasting yarn. Sl 5 loops below thumb opening and 4 loops above opening to needles. Pick up 2 sts at each corner of thumb opening. Divide 13 sts on 3 needles and work even until thumb is long enough.

Thumb Decrease:
Rnd 1: (P 1, p 2 tog) around ending with p 1 (9).
Rnd 2: P 2 tog around, ending with p 1 (5).
Draw yarn through 5 remaining sts, pull tight and fasten.

LEFT MITTEN
Same as for right mitten except following:

Thumb Opening: Work 11 sts in rib pattern. With contrasting yarn, k next 5 sts. Sl these 5 sts back to left needle and k again with mitten yarn. Finish 17 sts of Rnd in rib pattern. Remainder of mitten is same as for right mitten.

For cord, see directions for Looped Cord (page 5). The 18-in cord for this mitten requires 4 yards of yarn. Thread finished cord through beading row, tie in bow.

Like little snowflakes in the sky...

Dots N' Dashes

Beginner

This snug little mitten is one of the easiest styles you could knit...and it's thumbless to keep tiny fingers warm.

Size: 5 inches.
Yarn: 1 oz Knitting Worsted Weight.
Needles: 1 pair single point in size needed to reach gauge, 1 pair two sizes smaller (for Two Needle Mittens); 1 set double point in size needed to reach gauge, 1 set two sizes smaller (for Four Needle Mittens).
Gauge: 5 stitches (sts) per inch.
Note: Pattern is the same for right and left mittens.

TWO NEEDLE MITTENS

Cuff: With smaller size needles cast on 26 sts. Work k 1, p 1 rib for 1½ ins or until cuff is as long as you wish.

Hand: Change to larger size needles and work in ss until mitten is 1/2 in less than desired finished length. End in p row, inserting marker in middle of last p row.

Decrease for Tip:
Row 1: K 2 tog, k to 2 sts before marker, k 2 tog, sl marker, k 2 tog, k to last 2 sts, k 2 tog (4 sts dec).
Row 2: P. Rep these two rows once more. Weave remaining 18 sts tog. Sew side seam of mitten.

FOUR NEEDLE MITTENS

Cuff: With smaller size needles cast on 26 sts. Divide on 3 needles, being careful not to twist. Work k 1, p 1 rib for 1½ ins or until cuff is as long as you wish.

Hand: Change to larger size needles and work in ss until mitten is 1/2 in less than desired finished length. Insert markers to indicate end and midpoint of Rnd.

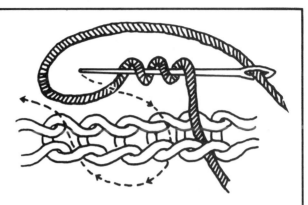

Dots N' Dashes Design: This design is worked in 3 vertical rows of French Knots and 2 rows of running stitches, done in contrasting colors of Knitting Worsted. For the French Knot, draw your needle to right side of the mitten in center stitch, the third row above ribbing. Wind the yarn around needle 3 times. Pass your needle to the wrong side in next stitch above (see above drawing). This is 1 French Knot completed. Repeat every 3 rows 6 times more. Work a row of running stitches on either side of the French Knots with the yarn passing over 2 cross threads and under 1 cross thread (see drawing below). Work additional rows of 6 French Knots along the outside of running stitches.

CROSSTHREADS

Decrease for Tip:
Rnd 1: K 2 tog, k to 2 sts before first marker, k 2 tog. Sl marker, k 2 tog, k to last 2 sts of Rnd, k 2 tog (4 sts dec).
Rnd 2: Work even. Rep these two Rnds once more. Weave remaining 18 sts tog.

It's a natural for good looks...

Double Seed Stitch

Little folks know being comfortable is something to smile about. This common stitch makes a mitten great for dressing up... or for casual wear.

Size: 6 inches.
Yarn: 2 oz Knitting Worsted Weight.
Needles: 1 pair single point in size needed to reach gauge, 1 pair two sizes smaller.
Gauge: 5 stitches (sts) per inch.

RIGHT MITTEN

Cuff: With smaller needles cast on 30 sts.
Row 1: *K in back loop, p 1. Rep from * to end of row.
Row 2: *K 1, p 1. Rep from * to end of row.
Rep these two rows until cuff measures 2 ins or is as long as you wish, ending with row 2. Inc in last st (31).

Hand: Change to larger size needles.
Row 1: K 15 (k 2, p 2) 4 times.
Row 2: (K 2, p 2) 4 times, p 15.
Row 3: K 15, (p 2, k 2) 4 times.
Row 4: (P 2, k 2) 4 times, p 15.
Rep above 4 rows until mitten measures approximately 2 ins above ribbing, ending with row 4.

Thumb Opening: K 5, sl these 5 sts to holder, k 10 *k 2, p 2. Rep from * to end of row. In next row: (K 2, p 2) 4 times, p 10, cast on 5 sts.
Resume 4 row pattern beg with row 3. Rep pattern until mitten is 1 in shorter than desired finished length, ending with row 4 of pattern.

Decrease for Tip:
Row 1: SSK, k 11, k 2 tog, SSK, (p 2, k 2) 3 times, k 2 tog (27).
Row 2: K 1, (p 2, k 2) 3 times, p to end of row.
Row 3: SSK, k 9, k 2 tog, SSK, k 1, (p 2, k 2) twice, p 1, k 2 tog (23).
Row 4: (K 2, p 2) 3 times, p 11.
Row 5: SSK, k 7, k 2 tog, SSK, k 8, k 2 tog (19).
Row 6: P 2 tog, p to end of row (18).
Weave remaining 18 sts tog.

Thumb: Sl 5 thumb sts from holder to left needle, join yarn, pick up 2 sts from corner of thumb opening and pick up 5 sts from cast-on edge above thumb opening. Work even in ss on these 12 thumb sts until thumb is long enough, ending with p row.

Thumb Decrease: K 2 tog across row. Draw yarn through 6 remaining sts, pull tight and sew thumb seam. Sew side seam of mitten.

LEFT MITTEN

Same as right mitten through cuff.

Hand: Change to larger size needles.
Row 1: (K 2, p 2) 4 times, k 15.
Row 2: P 15, (k 2, p 2) 4 times.
Row 3: (P 2, k 2) 4 times, k 15.
Row 4: P 15, (p 2, k 2) 4 times. Work to correspond to right mitten up to thumb opening. To reverse thumb position work thumb opening as follows: (K 2, p 2) 4 times, k 10, sl last 5 sts to holder for thumb. Cast on 5 sts.
Next row: P 15, (k 2, p 2) 4 times.
Resume 4 row pattern beg with row 3 and finish mitten to correspond to right mitten.

Left Thumb: With right side of mitten toward you, pick up 5 sts along cast-on edge above thumb opening. Pick up 2 sts at corner of thumb opening. Sl 5 sts from holder to left needle and knit them (12). Work in ss and finish to correspond to right thumb.

A special way to say "Be Mine"...

Scandinavian Valentine

Brighten up winter with these cute and cheery lover's hearts.

Size: 6 inches.
Yarn: Knitting Worsted Weight, 1 oz each Colors A and B.
Needles: 1 pair single point in size needed to reach gauge.
Gauge: 5 stitches (sts) per inch.

RIGHT MITTEN

Cuff: With Color A cast on 30 sts. Work Quaker Rib as follows:
Row 1: P.
Row 2: K.
Row 3: P.
Row 4: P.
Row 5: K.
Row 6: P.
Rep these 6 rows once more, then work rows 1, 2, 3 and 4 again. Rest of mitten is worked in ss following chart for color design.

Hand: Work even through row 14.

Thumb Opening:
Row 15: Work 5 sts from chart and sl to holder. Work remainder of row from chart.
Row 16: Work 25 sts from chart. Cast on 5 sts in Color B.

Finish Hand: Work rows 17-25 from chart.

Decrease for Tip:
Color design: Work first st, 2 center sts and last st in each row in Color B, remainder of sts in Color A.
Row 26: P 1, p 2 tog, p 9, p 2 tog, p 2, p 2 tog, p 9, p 2 tog, p 1 (26).
Row 27: K 1, k 2 tog, k 7, k 2 tog, k 2, k 2 tog, k 7, k 2 tog, k 1 (22).
Row 28: P 1, p 2 tog, p 5, p 2 tog, p 2, p 2 tog, p 5, p 2 tog, p 1 (18).
Weave remaining 18 sts tog.

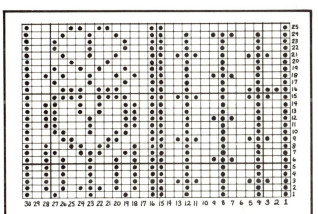

To knit this color pattern, simply work the mittens in stockinette stitch beginning in lower right corner.

Thumb: Sl 5 sts from holder to left needle and k with Color B. Pick up one st at corner of thumb and pick up 5 sts at cast-on edge above thumb opening. Work even on 11 sts until thumb is long enough, ending with p row.

Thumb Decrease: K 2 tog across row ending with k 1. Draw yarn through 6 remaining sts, draw tight, sew thumb seam and mitten side seam.

LEFT MITTEN

Same as for right mitten through row 14. To read chart for left mitten begin at center, read left half, then right half of each row.

Thumb Opening:
Row 15: Work 25 sts from chart. Sl last 5 sts in row to holder for thumb. Cast on 5 sts with Color B.
Row 16: Follow chart for entire row.
Rows 17-28 and weave tip same for right mitten.

Thumb: With right side of work towards you, pick up 5 sts with Color B on cast-on edge above thumb opening, pick up 1 st at corner of thumb. Sl 5 sts from holder to left needle and k them. Rest of thumb is same as for right mitten.

Advanced

A simple fashion accent for active kids...

Hidden Rib

Why is this mitten called the "Hidden Rib?" Because when you take it off, the ribs disappear! In addition, it's super warm!

Size: 6 inches.
Yarn: 2 oz Knitting Worsted Weight.
Needles: 1 pair single point in size needed to reach gauge, 1 pair two sizes smaller.
Gauge: 5 stitches (sts) per inch.

RIGHT MITTEN

Cuff: With smaller size needles, cast on 30 sts.
Row 1: *K 2, p 1. Rep from * to end of row.
Row 2: *K 1, p 2. Rep from * to end of row.
Rep above 2 rows until ribbing measures 1½ ins, ending with row 2.

Wrist:
Row 1: *K 1, p 2 tog. Rep from * to end of row (20).
Row 2: *K 1 in back loop, p 1. Rep from * to end of row.
Rep row 2 for 1 in.

Hand: Change to larger size needles. You should now be working on right side (the k 2, p 1 side of cuff). If not, rep row 2 of wrist 1 more time.
Row 1: *K 1, k in front and back of next st. Rep from * to end of row (30).
Row 2: *K 1, p 2. Rep from * to end of row.
Row 3: *K 2, p 1. Rep from * to end of row.
Rep rows 2 and 3 until mitten measures 3¾ ins. End with row 2.

Thumb Opening:
Row 1: K 2, p 1, k 2. Sl these 5 sts to holder. Continue row as follows: P 1, *k 2, p 1. Rep from * to end of row.
Row 2: *K 1, p 2. Rep from * 7 times more, k 1, cast on 5 sts (30).
Row 3: *K 2, p 1. Rep from * to end of row.
Row 4: *K 1, p 2. Rep from * to end of row.
Rep above rows 3 and 4 until mitten measures 1 in less than desired length, ending with row 4.

Tip Decrease:
Row 1: *K 1, SSK, k 2, p 1. Rep from * to end of row (25).
Row 2: *K 1, p 4. Rep from * to end of row.
Row 3: *K 3, SSK. Rep from * to end of row (20).
Row 4: P 20. Weave remaining 20 sts tog.

Thumb: Sl 5 thumb sts from holder to right needle. Join yarn and pick up 2 sts at corner of thumb opening, pick up 5 sts along cast on sts above thumb opening (12). Work in ss until thumb is long enough, ending with p row.

Thumb Decrease: K 2 tog across row. Draw yarn through 6 remaining sts, pull tight, sew thumb seam and side seam of mitten.

LEFT MITTEN

Same as for right mitten except following:

Thumb Opening:
Row 1: *K 2, p 1. Rep from * 7 times more, k 1. Sl remaining 5 sts to holder. Cast on 5 sts on right needle.
Row 2: *K 1, p 2. Rep from * to end of row. Continue to work mitten tip to correspond to right mitten.

Thumb: With right side of mitten toward you, pick up 5 sts along cast-on edge above thumb opening. Pick up 2 sts at corner of thumb opening. Sl 5 sts from holder to left needle and k them. Work in ss and finish to correspond to right mitten.

Advanced

Reach into your bag of yarn scraps for a lovely...

Sampler

This is just the mitten to show off your knitting techniques. Let different colors and stitches steal the show!

Size: 6 inches.
Yarn: Knitting Worsted Weight, 2/3 oz each of Colors A, B and C.
Needles: 1 pair single point in size needed to reach gauge, 1 pair two sizes smaller.
Gauge: 5 stitches (sts) per inch.

RIGHT MITTEN

Cuff: With smaller size needles cast on 30 sts with Color A.
Row 1: K 1, p 2 across.
Row 2: K 2, p 1 across.
Rep these 2 rows until cuff measures 2¼ ins or is as long as you wish, ending with row 2.

Hand: Change to larger size needles and k 6 rows in Color B. Work next 1 in with Color C in ss, ending with a p row. Change to Color A.
Row 1: K.
Row 2: *K 1, sl 1 as if to p, with yarn behind work. Rep from * across.
Row 3: K.
Row 4: *K 2, sl 1 as if to p with yarn behind work. Rep from * across.
Rep rows 1 and 2 once more.
With Color B, work even in ss until mitten reaches angle made by thumb and index finger.

Thumb Opening: K 6 sts and sl to holder. K 24. Next row, p 24, cast on 6 sts. Work 2 more rows in ss.

Finish Hand: Change to Color C.
Row 1: K 1, *yo, k 2, pass yo over 2 k sts. Rep from * across ending with k 1.
Row 2: P.
Rep these 2 rows twice more. Change to Color A, work even in ss until mitten is ¾ in less than desired finished length. End with a p row and insert marker in center of last row.

Tip Decrease:
Row 1: K 1, SSK, k to 3 sts before marker, k 2 tog, k 1, sl marker, k 1, SSK, k to last 3 sts in row, k 2 tog, k 1 (4 sts dec).
Row 2: P.
Rep above 2 rows once more. Weave remaining 22 sts tog.

Thumb: Sl 6 sts from holder to right needle. Join Color B, pick up 1 st in corner of thumb opening and 5 sts at cast-on edge above thumb opening. Work even on 12 thumb sts in ss until thumb is long enough, ending with a p row.

Thumb Decrease: K 2 across. Draw yarn through remaining 6 sts, pull tight and sew thumb seam and side seam of mitten.

LEFT MITTEN

Same as right mitten except following:

Thumb Opening: K 24, sl remaining 6 sts to holder. Cast on 6 sts. Next row, p 30. Work 2 more rows in ss.

Thumb: With right side of work towards you, pick up 5 sts at cast-on edge above thumb opening, pick up 1 st at corner of thumb opening, sl 6 sts from holder to left needle and k them (12). Finish thumb as for right mitten.

The "prettiest pretender" of them all...

Zig Zag Chain

Beginner

This simple looped chain stitch is so lovely people will think it's a difficult, knit-in design. But it's easy to knit!

Size: 7 inches.
Yarn: 2 oz Knitting Worsted Weight.
Needles: 1 pair single point in size needed to reach gauge, 1 pair two sizes smaller (for Two Needle Mittens); 1 set double point in size needed to reach gauge, 1 set two sizes smaller (for Four Needle Mittens).
Gauge: 5 stitches (sts) per inch.
Note: Pattern is the same for right and left mittens.

TWO NEEDLE MITTENS

Cuff: With smaller size needles cast on 34 sts. Work in k 1, p 1 rib for 2 ins or until cuff is as long as you wish. Rest of mitten is worked in ss.

Hand: Change to larger size needles and work even for 1 in. End with p row.

Thumb Gore:
Row 1: K 16 sts, place marker, inc in each of next 2 sts, place second marker. K remaining 16 sts.
Row 2: P.
Row 3: Inc after first marker and before second marker.
Rep rows 2 and 3 until there are 12 sts between markers. Work even until mitten reaches angle of thumb and index finger. End with a p row.

Thumb: K to marker. Sl these 16 sts to holder. K to next marker, cast on 1 st. Sl remaining 16 sts to second holder. P back on thumb sts, cast on 1 more st. Work even on 14 thumb sts until thumb is long enough, ending with p row.

Thumb Decrease:
Row 1: K 2 tog across row.
Row 2: P.

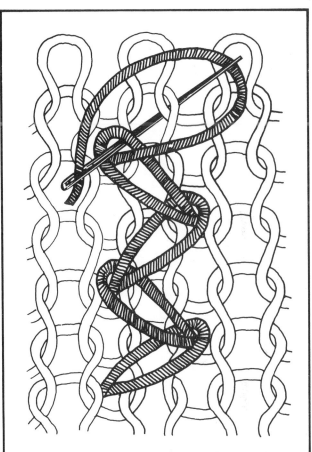

Zig Zag Chain Design: Work 3 rows of this zig zag chain stitch on the back of the mitten. Use contrasting colors, or the same color as the mitten yarn, as shown. Thread the yarn into a blunt tapestry needle and bring it to the outside of the mitten, just to the left of the center stitch in the first row above the ribbing. Form a loop by reinserting the needle into the original hole, and come out again just to the right of the center stitch in the third row (see drawing). Draw the yarn only until a gentle loop is formed. Repeat, working on alternate diagonals. Stop 8 rows below the tip of the mitten. Work additional rows of chains, 3 stitches on either side of the first row. Work until 3 rows from tip of mitten. Fasten ends on inside.

CONTINUED ON PAGE 48

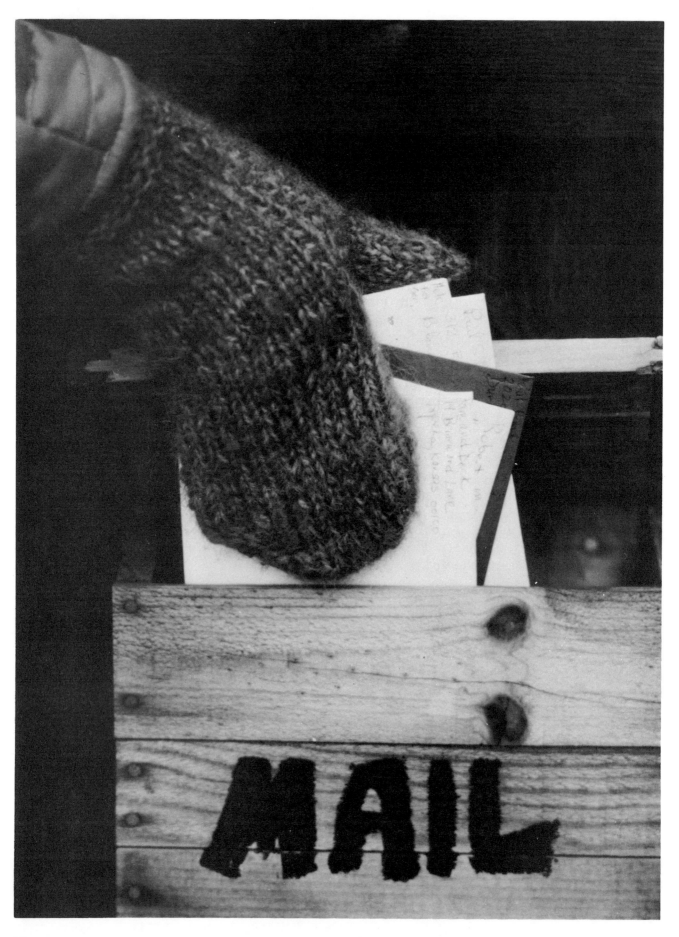

A soft—but oh-so flattering—mitten look...

Mohair Plus

Here's a beauty that's surprisingly warm because it's knit with double strands of mohair and sportweight yarn. And so feminine!

Size: 8 inches.
Yarn: 1½ oz Mohair, 2 oz Sportweight.
Needles: 1 pair single point in size needed to reach gauge.
Gauge: With mohair and sport yarn worked together, 3½ stitches (sts) per inch.
Note: Entire mitten is worked with double strand, one of mohair and one of sport yarn.

RIGHT MITTEN
Cuff: Cast on 28 sts. K each row for 2 ins.

Hand: Remainder of mitten is done in ss. Work even until entire mitten measures 5½ ins, ending with a p row.

Thumb Opening:
Row 1: K 7 sts, sl these 7 sts to holder. K 21.
Row 2: P 21, cast on 7 sts.

Finish Hand: Work even until mitten is 1¾ ins shorter than desired finished length, ending with a p row.

Decrease for Tip:
Row 1: *K 2 tog, k 10, k 2 tog. Rep from * (24).
Row 2: P.
Row 3: *K 2 tog, k 8, k 2 tog. Rep from * (20).
Row 4: P.
Row 5: *K 2 tog, k 6, k 2 tog. Rep from * (16).
Row 6: P.
Row 7: *K 2 tog, k 4, k 2 tog. Rep from * (12).
Row 8: P.
Weave remaining 12 sts tog.

Thumb: Sl 7 thumb sts from holder to left needle, join yarn and k them. Pick up 1 st at corner of thumb opening and pick up 6 sts from cast-on edge above thumb opening. Work even on 14 sts until thumb is long enough, ending with a p row.

Thumb Decrease:
Row 1: K 2 tog across row (7).
Row 2: P.
Row 3: K 2 tog across row ending with k 1.
Draw yarn through remaining 4 sts, pull tight and sew thumb seam. Sew side seam of mitten.

LEFT MITTEN
Same as for right mitten except following:

Thumb Opening:
Row 1: K 21, sl last 7 sts to holder for thumb. Cast on 7 sts.
Row 2: P.
Continue as for right mitten.

Thumb: With right side of work toward you, join yarn and pick up 6 sts along cast-on edge above thumb opening. Pick up 1 st at corner of thumb. Sl 7 thumb sts from holder to left needle and k them. Rest of mitten is same as for right mitten.

As colorful as a box of melted crayons...

Rainbow Delight

Got leftover yarn? Not only will this mitten use up your odds and ends of leftover yarn, but it will look good with every coat, hat and scarf your teen-agers own!

Size: 7 inches.
Yarn: Leftover yarn scraps to equal 2 oz.
Needles: 1 set double point in size needed to reach gauge, 1 set two sizes smaller.
Gauge: 5 stitches (sts) per inch.

RIGHT MITTEN

Hem: With smaller size needles cast on 34 sts. Divide on 3 double pointed needles, being careful not to twist. Work in ss for ¾ in. P one Rnd for sharp crease on hem.

Cuff and Hand: Change to larger size needles and work even in ss until mitten reaches angle of thumb and index finger.

Thumb Opening: With contrasting yarn k 6 sts and sl these 6 sts back to left needle; k them again with mitten yarn. Continue working even until mitten is 1 in less than desired finished length.

Tip Decrease: Rearrange sts on needles as follows: 17, 9, 8. First st of 17 is directly above right end of thumb opening.
Rnd 1: K 1, SSK, k to last 3 sts on first needle, k 2 tog, k 1. Second and third needles: K 1, SSK, k to last 3 sts of Rnd, k 2 tog, k 1.
Rnd 2: K.
Rep above 2 Rnds twice more. Sl sts from second needle to third and weave remaining 22 sts tog.

Thumb: Remove contrasting yarn. Sl 6 loops below thumb opening to first needle. Divide 5 loops above opening on second and third needles. Work even in ss, picking up 1 st at each corner of thumb opening on first Rnd, until thumb is long enough (13).

Thumb Decrease: K 2 tog around ending with k 1. Draw yarn through remaining 7 sts, pull tight and fasten.

LEFT MITTEN
Same as for right mitten except following:

Decrease for Tip: Rearrange sts on needles as follows: 17, 9, 8. Last of 17 sts is directly above left end of thumb opening.

Show off a pretty hand...

Quaker Rib

The advantage of this simple mitten is it stretches as you put it on, for a warm and comfortable fit each time!

Size: 7 inches.
Yarn: 2 oz Knitting Worsted Weight.
Needles: 1 set double point in size needed to reach gauge, 1 set two sizes smaller.
Gauge: 5 stitches (sts) per inch.

RIGHT MITTEN

Cuff: With smaller size needles cast on 33 sts. Divide on 3 double pointed needles, being careful not to twist. (K 1 in back loop, p 2) around until cuff measures 2 ins.

Hand: Change to larger size needles. Inc 3 sts in next Rnd (36). Work in ss for 1¼ ins.

Rib Pattern:
Rnds 1, 2 and 3: P.
Rnds 4-8: K.
Rep these 8 Rnds once, then work 3 Rnds of p once more.

Thumb Opening: With contrasting yarn k 6 sts. Sl these 6 sts back to left needle and k them again with mitten yarn. K rest of Rnd. K 4 more Rnds. Work a p rib of 3 rows, k rib of 5 rows and another p rib.

Finish Hand: Remainder of mitten is worked in ss. Work even until mitten is 1 in less than desired finished length. Rearrange sts on needles as follows: 18, 9, 9. First st on the right of the 18 sts should be directly above right end of thumb opening.

Decrease for Tip:
Rnd 1: K 1, SSK, k to last 3 sts of first needle, k 2 tog, k 1. K 1, SSK on second needle, k to last 3 sts on third needle, k 2 tog, k 1. (Dec 4 sts).
Rnd 2: K. Rep these 2 Rnds twice more. Sl sts from second needle to third needle. Weave remaining 24 sts together

Thumb: Remove contrasting yarn from thumb sts. Sl 6 loops below thumb opening to 1 needle. Divide 5 loops above opening on second and third needle. Work thumb in ss, picking up 1 st in each corner of thumb opening on first Rnd (13). Work even until thumb is long enough.

Thumb Decrease: K 2 tog around ending with k 1 (7). Draw yarn through these last 7 sts, pull tight and fasten.

LEFT MITTEN

Pattern is the same for left hand except the following:

Finish Hand: Rearrange sts on needles as follows: 18, 9, 9. Last st on the left of the 18 sts should be directly above left end of thumb opening.

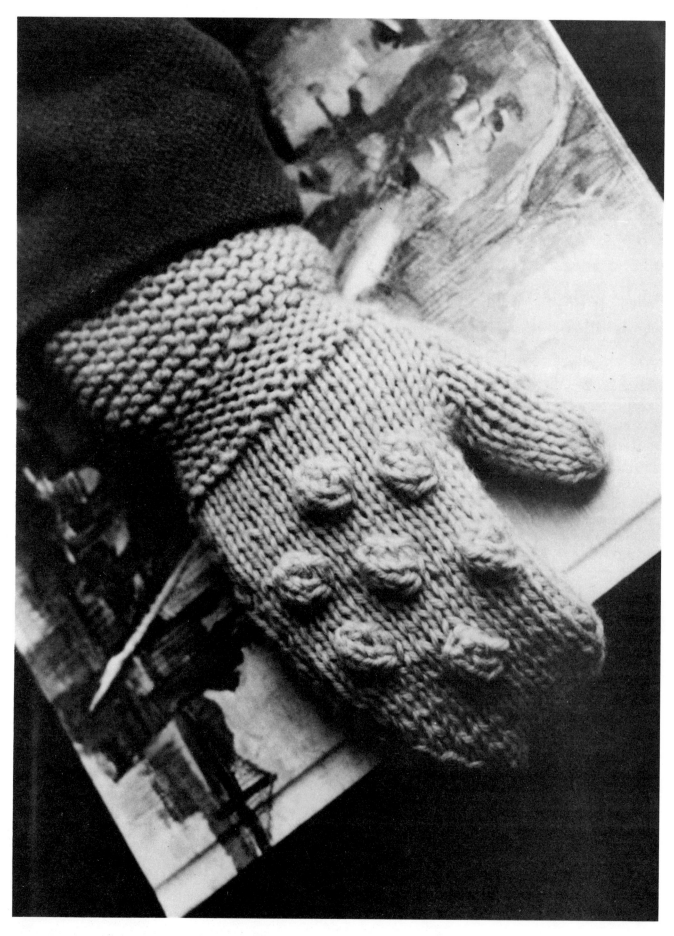

Just the right amount of elegance...

Bobble Back

Look like popcorn stitches? Better yet, these are bobbles—bigger and better and easy to knit.

Size: 7 inches.
Yarn: 2 oz Knitting Worsted Weight.
Needles: 1 pair single point in size needed to reach gauge, 1 pair two sizes smaller.
Gauge: 5 stitches (sts) per inch.

RIGHT MITTEN

Cuff: With larger size needles cast on 39 sts. K every row until cuff measures 2 ins.

Decrease for Wrist: Change to smaller size needles. (K 2, k 2 tog) 9 times, ending with k 1, k 2 tog (29). K every row for 1 in.

Increase for Hand: Change to larger size needles (K 4, inc in next st) 5 times ending with k 4 (34). Rest of mitten is worked in ss.

Hand: For design on back sts work bobble st where indicated by "X" on chart as follows: (yo, k 1, yo, k 1) all in 1 st. Turn and work in ss on 4 bobble sts for 4 rows. Now pass 3 sts over the st just completed.

Thumb Gore: Thumb gore is worked as follows beg with next row:
Row 1: K 16, insert marker, k 2, insert second marker, k 16. Sts between markers are thumb sts.
Row 2: P.
Row 3: K 16, inc in each of next 2 sts, k 16 (36).
Row 4: P.
Inc after first marker and before second marker every k row working even on every p row until there are 12 sts between markers. End with p row. This will be row 12. First bobble is worked in ninth st of row 9 as indicated on chart. Continue to follow chart for placement of additional bobbles on back sts.

Thumb: Row 13 (as in chart): K 4, bobble, k 7, bobble, k 3 and sl these 16 sts to holder. K 12 thumb sts, cast on 1 st, sl remaining 16 sts to holder. P 13 thumb sts, cast on 1 st (14). Work even until thumb is long enough, ending with a p row.

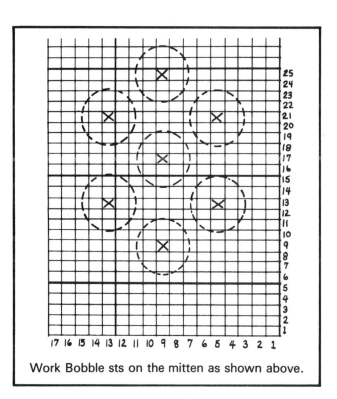

Work Bobble sts on the mitten as shown above.

Thumb Decrease: K 2 tog across (7). Draw yarn through remaining 7 sts, pull tight and sew thumb seam.

Finish Hand: Sl 16 sts from first holder to right needle. Join yarn, pick up 2 sts from base of thumb seam, sl remaining 16 sts to left needle, and resuming row 13, k them (34). Work even through row 25, working bobbles as indicated on chart. After last bobble, continue working even until mitten is 1¼ ins less than desired finished length, ending with a p row, and inserting marker in center of last row.

Decrease for Tip:
Row 1: K 1, SSK, k to 3 sts before marker, k 2 tog, k 1, sl marker, k 1, SSK, k to last 3 sts in row, k 2 tog, k 1 (4 sts dec).
Row 2: P.
Rep these 2 rows twice more. Weave remaining 22 sts tog.

LEFT MITTEN

Pattern is the same as for right mitten except the following: Positions of back and palm sts are reversed. On odd numbered rows palm sts are worked first, then thumb sts, then back sts with bobbles. Remainder of mitten is the same.

A wonderful, "luck of the Irish" style...

Ring Cable Fisherknit

Advanced

There's plenty of knitting detail here to make both knitter and wearer happy.

Size: 8 inches.
Yarn: 4 oz Knitting Worsted Weight.
Needles: 1 set double point in size needed to reach gauge, 1 set double point two sizes smaller for ribbing.
Gauge: 6 stitches (sts) per inch.

RIGHT MITTEN

Cuff: On smaller needles, cast on 48 sts. Divide on 3 needles being careful not to twist sts. Work in rib of k 1, p 1 for 2½ ins or until cuff is as long as you wish. On last Rnd inc in 12th and 13th sts of Rnd (50).

Hand: Change to larger size needles and work 8 Rnd pattern on 26 back sts as follows:
Rnd 1: P 2, k 1, p 2, k 1, p 3, k 8, p 3, k 1, p 2, k 1, p 2, k 24. (Note: 24 palm sts are k throughout pattern).
Rnd 2: P 2, k 1, p 2, k 1, p 3, k 8, p 3, k 1, p 2, k 1, p 2.
Rnd 3: P 3, k 2, p 4, sl next 2 sts to cable needle and leave at front, p 2, k 2 from cable needle, sl next 2 sts to cable needle and leave at back, k 2, p 2 from cable needle, p 4, k 2, p 3.
Rnd 4: P 3, k 2, p 6, k 4, p 6, k 2, p 3.
Rnd 5: P 2, k 1, p 2, k 1, p 5, k 4, p 5, k 1, p 2, k 1, p 2.
Rnd 6: P 2, k 1, p 2, k 1, p 5, k 4, p 5, k 1, p 2, k 1, p 2.
Rnd 7: P 3, k 2, p 4, sl next 2 sts to cable needle and leave at back, k 2, k 2 from cable needle, sl next 2 sts to cable needle and leave at front, k 2, k 2 sts from cable needle, p 4, k 2, p 3.
Rnd 8: P 3, k 2, p 4, k 8, p 4, k 2, p 3.

Thumb Gore: Rep above 8 Rnds twice more. At the same time work thumb gore on 24 palm sts beg with Rnd 9 as follows:
Rnd 9: After working 26 pattern sts, k 2, insert marker, inc in each of next 2 sts, insert second marker, k 20.
Rnd 10: Work even, maintaining pattern on back sts.
Rnd 11: Inc after first marker and before second marker.
Rep last 2 Rnds until there are 18 sts between markers at end of 24th Rnd.

Thumb:
Rnd 25: Work 26 back sts as for Rnd 1 of pattern. K 2 palm sts. Sl these 28 sts to a holder. Cast on 1 st, k 18 thumb sts, cast on 1 st. Sl remaining 20 palm sts to second holder.
Divide 20 thumb sts on 3 needles. Work in ss until thumb is long enough.

Decrease Thumb Tip:
Rnd 1: K 2 tog (10).
Rnd 2: K 2 tog (5).
Thread yarn through remaining 5 sts, pull tight and fasten.

Finish Hand: Sl 2 palm sts from first holder to right needle. Join yarn. Pick up 2 sts from base of thumb. Sl 8 of the palm sts from second holder to needle and k. Sl remaining 12 palm sts from holder to second needle and k. Sl 26 back sts from holder to needle.
Work even beg with Rnd 2 of 8 Rnd pattern. Rep 8 Rnds until you have a total of 48 Rnds counting from ribbing.
Rnd 49: P 2, k 4, p 3, k 8, p 3, k 4, p 2.
Rnd 50: P 2, k 4, p 3, k 8, p 3, k 4, p 2.
Rnd 51: P 2 tog, k 4, p 3, sl next 2 sts to cable needle and leave in front, p 2, k 2 sts from cable needle, sl next 2 sts to cable needle and leave at back, k 2, p 2 sts from cable needle, p 3, k 4, p 2 tog (48).
Rnd 52: P 1, k 4, p 3, k 3, p 2, k 3, p 3, k 4, p 1.
Rep Rnd 52 until mitten measures 1¼ ins less than desired length. Then begin dec for tip.

Decrease for Tip:
Rnd 1: Back sts—K 2 tog, continue working in rib pattern as established in previous Rnd. K last 2 back sts tog.

CONTINUED ON PAGE 48

The perfect answer to long, frosty days and nights...

Rep Stripe

If snow always manages to somehow get inside your mittens, this bulky, long-cuffed mitten should be just what you've waited for.

Size: 8 inches.
Yarn: 2½ oz Knitting Worsted Weight of each of Colors A, B and C.
Needles: 1 pair single point in size needed to reach gauge.
Gauge: With double strand of Knitting Worsted used throughout, 3½ stitches (sts) per inch.

RIGHT MITTEN

Cuff: With double strand of Color A, cast on 31 sts. K 4 rows. Remainder of mitten is worked in ss, alternating 1 row each of Colors A, B and C. Colors are carried loosely along selvage. Work even until mitten measures 3¼ ins (including border), ending with a p row.

Decrease for Wrist: (K 3, k 2 tog) 6 times, ending with k 1 (25). Continue working even, without changing colors for 4 more rows.

Increase for Hand: Resume color sequence being sure to run next color up very loosely along selvage. Since this is a 7 row "jump" you may prefer to break that color and join again before beg next row: (K 7, inc in next st) 3 times, end with k 1 (28). Bring up next color loosely along selvage, or break off and join before working next row. Work even until mitten reaches angle made by thumb and index finger, ending with a p row.

Thumb Opening: K 6 sts and sl to holder. K remaining 22 sts. Next row: P 22, cast on 6 sts (28).

Finish Hand: Break off color needed for next row and join again above thumb opening. Work even until mitten is 2 ins shorter than desired finished length. Work even without changing colors for 1 in ending with a p row.

Decrease for Tip:
Row 1: (K 1, SSK, k 8, k 2 tog, k 1) twice (24).
Row 2: P.
Row 3: (K 1, SSK, k 6, k 2 tog, k 1) twice (20).
Row 4: P.
Row 5: (K 1, SSK, k 4, k 2 tog, k 1) twice (16).
Row 6: P.
Weave remaining 16 sts tog.

Thumb: Discontinue color sequence and work thumb in one color. Sl 6 sts from holder to left needle, join yarn and k them. Pick up 1 st in corner of thumb opening, pick up 5 sts at cast-on edge above thumb opening. Work even on 12 thumb sts until thumb is long enough, ending with a p row.

Thumb Decrease:
Row 1: (K 1, k 2 tog) four times (8).
Row 2: P 2 tog four times (4).
Draw yarn through 4 remaining sts, draw tight and sew thumb seam. Sew side seam of mitten.

LEFT MITTEN

Same as right mitten except following:

Thumb Opening:
Row 1: K 22, sl remaining 6 sts to holder. Cast on 6 sts.
Row 2: P.

Thumb: With right side of work towards you, pick up 5 sts at cast-on edge above thumb opening and pick up 1 st at corner. Sl 6 thumb sts from holder to left needle and k them. Rest of thumb is same as for right mitten.

Stylish, neat and versatile...

Seed Band Bulky

Who would think a bulky-yarn mitten could look so sleek? Its nice fitted cuff gives sure warmth and definite charm.

Size: 7 inches.
Yarn: 4 oz Bulky.
Needles: 1 set double point in size needed to reach gauge.
Gauge: 3½ stitches (sts) per inch.

RIGHT MITTEN

Cuff: Cast on 26 sts. Divide sts on 3 needles (9, 9, 8).
Rnd 1: K 1, p 1 around.
Rnd 2: P 1, k 1 around.
Rep these 2 Rnds twice more. Remainder of mitten is in ss. Work even for 1¼ ins.

Decrease for Wrist:
Rnd 1: K 3, SSK, (k 2, SSK) 4 times, k 3, SSK (20). Work even for 3 Rnds.
Rnd 5: K 3, inc, (K 2, inc) 4 times, k 3, inc (26). Work even until mitten reaches angle made by index finger and thumb.

Thumb Opening:
Rnd 1: With contrasting yarn, k next 5 sts. Sl these 5 sts back to left needle and k again with mitten yarn. Continue working even until mitten is 1 in shorter than desired length.

Decrease for Tip: Divide sts on needles as follows: 13 sts on first needle. The first of these 13 sts is to the immediate right of thumb opening; 7 sts on second needle, 6 on third needle.
Rnd 1: *SSK, k 9, k 2 tog. Rep from * (22).
Rnd 2: Work even.
Rnd 3: *SSK, k 7, k 2 tog. Rep from * (18).
Rnd 4: Work even.
Rnd 5: *SSK, k 5, k 2 tog. Rep from * (14).
Rnd 6: Work even.
Sl sts from third needle to second needle. You will have 16 sts divided evenly on two needles. Weave tog.

Thumb: Remove contrasting yarn. Join mitten yarn, sl 5 loops below thumb opening to needle and k. With second needle, pick up 1 st in left corner of opening, and 2 of the loops above thumb opening. With third needle pick up last 2 loops above thumb opening and 1 st in right corner. Work even on these 11 thumb sts until thumb is long enough.

Thumb Decrease: K 2 tog around, ending with k 1. Draw yarn through 6 remaining sts, pull tight and fasten.

LEFT MITTEN

Same as for right mitten up to dec for tip.

Divide sts for left mitten as follows: 13 on first needle. The last of these 13 sts is to the immediate left of the thumb opening; 7 sts go on second needle, 6 on third. Rest of pattern is identical to right mitten.

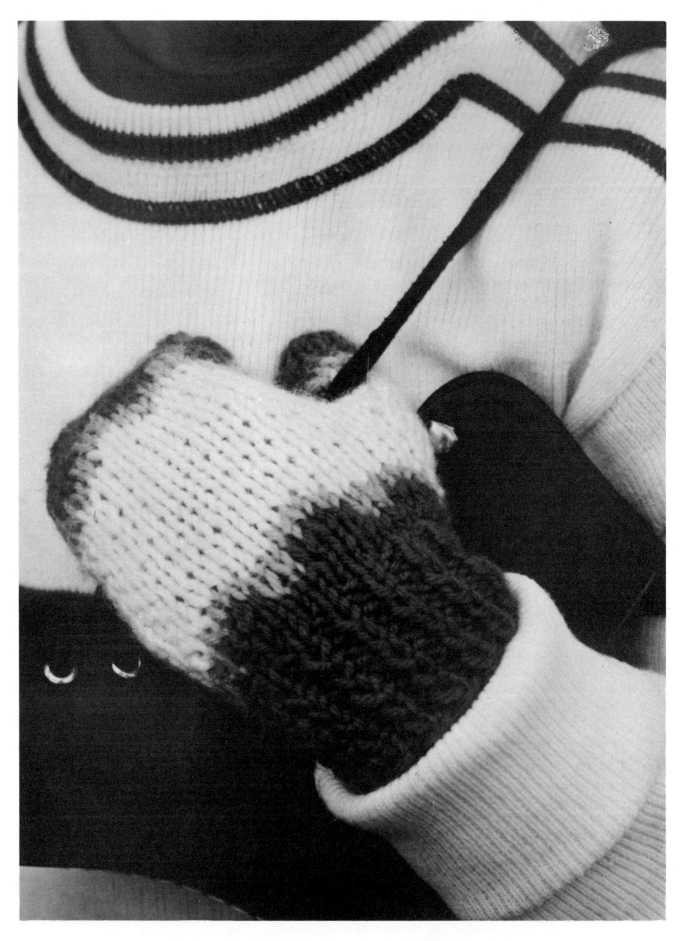

Discover a kicky, sure-hit mitten project...

Intermediate

Scandinavian Stripe

With whatever three-color combination you like, this sporty mitten will be someone's special favorite all winter long.

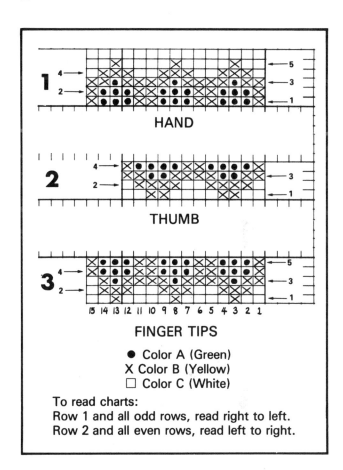

Size: 6 inches.
Yarn: Knitting Worsted Weight, 1 oz each Colors A, B, C.
Needles: 1 pair single point in size needed to reach gauge, 1 pair two sizes smaller.
Gauge: 5 stitches (sts) per inch.
Note: Pattern is the same for right and left mittens.

Cuff: With smaller needles and Color A, cast on 30 sts. Work in rib of k 1, p 1 for 1¾ ins or until cuff is as long as you wish.

Hand: Change to large size needles. K 1 row and p 1 row in Color A. Continue in ss working from Chart 1 for next 6 rows.

Thumb Gore:
Row 7: Continuing with Color C, k 14, insert marker, inc in each of next 2 sts, insert second marker, k 14 (32).
Row 8: P.
Row 9: Inc after first marker and before second marker (34).
Rep rows 8 and 9 until there are 10 thumb sts between markers. Work even until mitten reaches angle of thumb and index finger, ending with a p row.

Thumb: K 14, sl these 14 sts to holder. Pick up one st at right of thumb sts, k 10 thumb sts, pick up 1 st at left of thumb sts. Sl last 14 sts to second holder. P back on 12 thumb sts. Work even in ss following 4 rows of Chart 2. Continue with Color A until thumb is long enough, ending with p row.

Thumb Decrease: K 2 tog across row. Draw yarn through remaining 6 sts, pull tight and sew thumb seam.

Finish Hand: Sl 14 sts from first holder to right needle. Join Color C and pick up 2 sts from base of thumb seam. Sl remaining 14 sts from second holder to left needle and k them (30). Work even until mitten is 1¾ ins less than desired finished length, ending with p row. Work the next 5 rows from Chart 3.
Next row: P with Color A inserting marker in middle of row.

Decrease for Tip:
Row 1: SSK, k to 2 sts before marker, k 2 tog, sl marker, SSK, k to last 2 sts in row, k 2 tog (26).
Row 2: P.
Rep these two rows twice more (22, 18). Weave remaining 18 sts tog. Sew side seam of mitten.

Set the mood with big, bold stripes...

Big Stripe Bulky

Beginner

There's nothing shy about this masculine mitten... and with plenty of color for a bleak, blustery day.

Size: 10 inches.
Yarn: Two, 2 oz skeins Bulky Color A, one, 2 oz skein Bulky Color B. (You may substitute 70 yards Knitting Worsted Weight [used double] for Color B.)
Needles: 1 pair single point in size needed to reach gauge, one pair two sizes smaller.
Gauge: 3½ stitches (sts) per inch.
Note: Pattern is the same for right and left mittens.

Cuff: With smaller size needles, cast on 35 sts.
Row 1: (P 1, k 1 in back loop) across row ending with p 1.
Row 2: (K 1, p 1) across row ending with k 1.
Rep rows 1 and 2 until cuff is 2½ ins or is as long as you wish, ending with row 2.

Hand: Remainder of mitten is worked in ss. Change to larger size needles inc in last st of first row (36). Work even for 1 in ending with p row and inserting markers in last row as follows: P 16, insert marker, p 4, insert second marker, p 16.

Thumb Gore:
Row 1: Inc after first marker and before second marker (38).
Rows 2, 3, 4, 5 and 6: Work even.
Row 7: Inc after first marker and before second marker (40).
Rows 8, 9 and 10: Work even.
Row 11: Inc after first marker and before second marker (42).
Row 12: Work even.
Continue to work even until mitten reaches angle of index finger and thumb, ending with a p row.

Thumb:
Row 1: K 16, sl these 16 sts to holder. With Color B, pick up one st at right of thumb gore, k next 10 thumb sts, pick up one st at left of thumb gore. Sl remaining 16 sts to holder. Work even on 12 thumb sts for 1½ ins. Change to Color A and work even until thumb is long enough, ending with p row.

Thumb Decrease:
Row 1: (K 1, k 2 tog) across row (8).
Row 2: P 2 tog across row (4). Draw yarn through remaining 4 sts, pull tight and sew thumb seam.

Finish Hand: Sl 16 sts from first holder to right needle. Join Color A yarn and pick up 4 sts from base of thumb seam. Sl remaining 16 sts from holder to left needle and k them (36). P next row. Break off Color A, join Color B and work even for 2 ins. Break off Color B and join Color A. Continue to work even until mitten is 1½ ins shorter than desired finished length. End with a p row.

Decrease for Tip:
Row 1: *K 1, SSK, k 12, k 2 tog, k 1. Rep from * (32).
Row 2: P.
Row 3: *K 1, SSK, k 10, k 2 tog, k 1. Rep from * (28).
Row 4: P.
Row 5: *K 1, SSK, k 8, k 2 tog, k 1. Rep from * (24).
Row 6: P.
Row 7: *K 1, SSK, k 6, k 2 tog, k 1. Rep from * (20).
Row 8: P.
Weave remaining 20 sts tog. Sew side seam of mitten.

Maximize the manly look...

Belted Band

Intermediate

An easy to knit mitten with the same strong look as a belt running through belt loops.

Size: 9 inches.
Yarn: 3 oz Knitting Worsted Weight.
Needles: 1 pair single point in size needed to reach gauge.
Gauge: 5 stitches (sts) per inch.
Note: Pattern is the same for right and left mittens.

Cuff: Cast on 50 sts.
Row 1: *(K 1, p 3) 6 times, k 1. Rep from *.
Row 2: *(P 1, k 3) 6 times, p 1. Rep from *.
Rep rows 1 and 2 until cuff measures 2½ ins or is as long as you wish, ending with row 2.

Decrease for Wrist:
Row 1: *(K 1, p 2 tog, p 1) 6 times, k 1. Rep from * (38).
Row 2: *(P 1, k 2) 6 times, p 1. Rep from *.
Row 3: *(K 1, p 2) 6 times, k 1. Rep from *.
Rep rows 2 and 3, then row 2 once more.

Increase for Hand:
Row 1: *(Inc in k st, p 2, k 1, p 2) 3 times. Inc in next st. Rep from * (46).
Row 2: P.
Begin thumb gore on next row.

Thumb Gore:
Row 1: K 21, insert marker, k 4, insert second marker, k 21.
Row 2: P.
Row 3: Inc after first marker and before second marker (48).
Rep rows 2 and 3 until there are 12 sts between markers. Work even until mitten reaches angle made by thumb and index finger, ending with a p row.

Thumb: K 21 sts and sl to holder. K 12 thumb sts, cast on 3 sts. Sl remaining 21 sts to holder. Next row, p 15 thumb sts, cast on 3 sts (18). Work even for 2 rows.

Rib Stripe:
Row 1: P 4, k 1, p 8, k 1, p 4.
Row 2: K 4, p 1, k 8, p 1, k 4.
Rep rows 1 and 2. Remainder of thumb is done in ss working even until thumb is long enough and ending with a p row.

Thumb Decrease:
Row 1: K 2 tog across row (9).
Row 2: P 2 tog across row ending with p 1 (5).
Draw yarn through remaining 5 sts, pull tight and sew thumb seam.

Finish Hand: Sl 21 sts from first holder to right needle. Join yarn, pick up 6 sts from base of thumb seam. Sl remaining 21 sts from second holder to left needle and k them (48). Work 2 rows even. Next row, (wrong side) p 2 tog, p 44, p 2 tog (46).

Rib Band:
Row 1: *(P 3, k 1) 5 times, p 3. Rep from *.
Row 2: *(K 3, p 1) 5 times, k 3. Rep from *.
Rep rows 1 and 2 three times more. Continue working even in ss for 1 in ending with p row. Rep rows 1 and 2 of Rib Band (above) twice. Work even in ss until mitten is 1½ ins less than desired finished length, ending with a p row.

Decrease for Tip:
Row 1: (K 1, SSK, k 17, k 2 tog, k 1) twice (42).
Row 2: P.
Row 3: (K 1, SSK, k 15, k 2 tog, k 1) twice (38).
Row 4: P.
Row 5: (K 1, SSK, k 13, k 2 tog, k 1) twice (34).
Row 6: P.
Row 7: (K 1, SSK, k 11, k 2 tog, k 1) twice (30).
Row 8: P.
Row 9: (K 1, SSK, k 9, k 2 tog, k 1) twice (26).
Row 10: P.
Weave remaining 26 sts tog. Sew side seam of mitten.

A classic look that stands out in a crowd...

Highland Plaid

Beginner

The perfect mitten for your favorite guy, with a simple worked on stem stitch...experiment.

Size: 11 inches.
Yarn: 4 oz Knitting Worsted Weight.
Needles: 1 pair single point in size needed to reach gauge, 1 pair two sizes smaller (for Two Needle Mittens); 1 set double point in size needed to reach gauge, 1 set two sizes smaller (for Four Needle Mittens).
Gauge: 5 stitches (sts) per inch.
Note: Pattern is the same for right and left mittens.

TWO NEEDLE MITTENS

Cuff: With smaller size needles cast on 54 sts. Work in k 1, p 1 rib for 2½ ins or until cuff is as long as you wish. Rest of mitten is worked in ss.

Hand: Change to larger size needles and work even for 1 in. End with p row.

Thumb Gore:
Row 1: K 26 sts, place marker, inc in each of next 2 sts, place second marker. K remaining 26 sts.
Row 2: P.
Row 3: Inc after first marker and before second marker.
Rep rows 2 and 3 until there are 18 sts between markers. Work even until mitten reaches angle of thumb and index finger. End with a p row.

Thumb: K to marker. Sl these 26 sts to holder. K to next marker, cast on 1 st. Sl remaining 26 sts to second holder. P back on thumb sts, cast on 1 more st. Work even on 20 thumb sts until thumb is long enough, ending with p row.

Thumb Decrease:
Row 1: K 2 tog across row.
Row 2: P.
Row 3: K 2 tog across row.

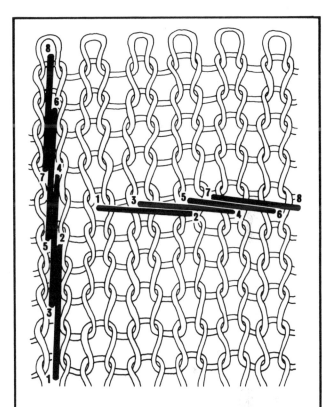

Highland Plaid Design: Even more exciting if placed off center! Make the lines in a stem stitch worked over 4 threads to the right and back under 2 threads to the left (see drawing). The vertical lines are 1½ stitches and 5½ stitches apart. The horizontal lines are 5 and 14 rows apart. Have fun experimenting with this spacing.

Draw yarn through remaining sts, pull tight and sew thumb seam.

Finish Hand: Sl 26 sts from first holder to right needle. Join yarn and pick up 2 sts from base of thumb seam, sl 26 sts from second holder to left needle and k them (54). Continue to work even until mitten is 1¾ ins less than finished length. End in p row, inserting marker in center of last p row.

Decrease for Tip:
Row 1: K 2 tog, k to 2 sts before marker, k 2 tog, sl marker, k 2 tog, k to last 2 sts, k 2 tog (4 sts dec).

CONTINUED ON PAGE 44

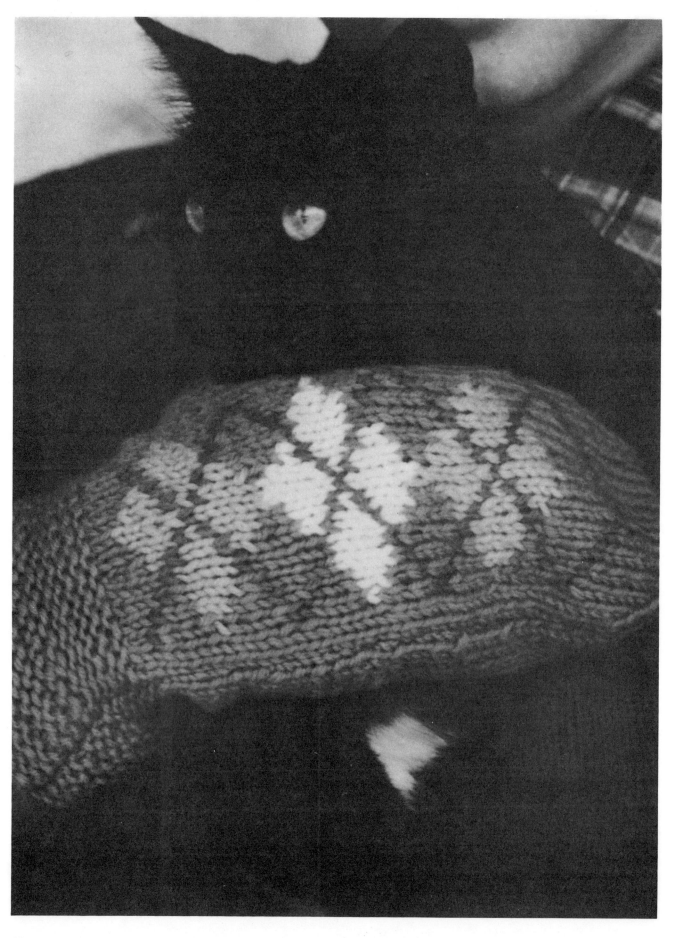

Remembering the fun of argyle socks...

Advanced

Argyle Nostalgia

Here's a pattern for advanced knitters, but what a great, classic mitten look! A pleasing, knit-in design.

Size: 8 inches.
Yarn: 3 oz Knitting Worsted Weight Color A, ½ oz each Colors B and C, 6 yards each Colors D and E.
Needles: 1 pair single point in size needed to reach gauge.
Gauge: 5 stitches (sts) per inch.

RIGHT MITTEN

Cuff: Cast on 40 sts in Color A. K each row until cuff measures 1¾ ins.

Decrease for Wrist: (K 2, k 2 tog) 10 times (30). K each row for ¾ ins more.

Increase for Hand:
Row 1: (K 2, inc in next st) 10 times (40).
Row 2: P.
Rest of mitten is worked in ss. Wind 1 bobbin of each color. Carry other colors behind crossbars of Colors D and E. All other colors are carried only up to adjoining colors where they are twisted to prevent holes.

Hand:
Row 1: Reading first row from chart (right to left) k following colors: 3 of A, 1 D, 5 A, 1 B, 5 A, 1 E, 4 A. Finish row with 20 palm sts k in Color A.
Row 2: P 20 sts. Next, reading row 2 of chart (left to right) p following colors: 5 A, 1 E, 3 A, 3 B, 3 A, 1 D, 4 A.
Continue to work even through row 8.

Thumb Gore:
Row 9: Work 19 sts from chart. Insert marker, inc in each of next 2 sts, insert second marker. K 19 (42).
Row 10: P 19 palm sts, 4 thumb sts, 19 back sts from chart.
Rows 11-20: Work 19 back sts from chart. Inc after

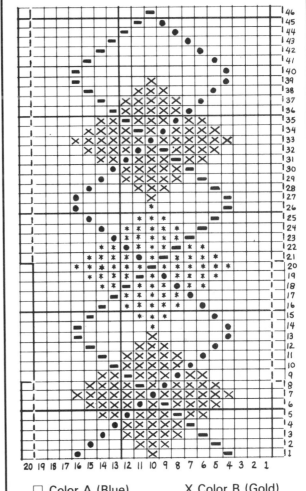

☐ Color A (Blue)   X Color B (Gold)
— Color D (Orange)   * Color C (White)
● Color E (Green)

Colors B and C should be knit as indicated on chart above. Dotted lines are for left mitten.

first marker and before second marker every k row until there are 14 sts between markers. P even numbered rows.

Thumb:
Row 21: Work 19 back sts from chart and sl to holder. K 14 thumb sts, cast on 1 st. Sl remaining 19 palm sts to second holder. P 15 thumb sts, cast on 1 st (16).

CONTINUED ON NEXT PAGE

43

ARGYLE NOSTALGIA:
CONTINUED FROM PREVIOUS PAGE

Work even on 16 thumb sts until thumb is long enough, ending with a p row.

Thumb Decrease:
Row 1: K 2 tog across (8).
Row 2: P 2 tog across (4).
Draw yarn through 4 remaining sts, pull tight and sew thumb seam.

Finish Hand: Sl 19 back sts from holder to right needle. Resuming row 21, join Color A and pick up 2 sts from base of thumb seam. Sl 19 palm sts to left needle and k them (40).
Row 22: P 20 palm sts and p 20 charted back sts.

Work even until mitten is 1¼ ins shorter than desired finished length. When end of chart is reached, continue in Color A. End with a p row, inserting marker in middle of last row.

Decrease for Tip:
Row 1: K 1, SSK, k to last 3 sts before marker, k 2 tog, k 1, sl marker, k 1, SSK, k to last 3 sts in row, k 2 tog, k 1 (4 sts dec).
Row 2: P.
Rep rows 1 and 2, three times more. Weave remaining 24 sts tog.

LEFT MITTEN
Pattern is the same except palm sts are worked first, then thumb gore, followed by back color design worked from chart.

HIGHLAND PLAID: CONTINUED FROM PAGE 41

Row 2: P.
Rep these two rows 5 times more. Weave remaining 30 sts tog. Sew side seam of mitten.

FOUR NEEDLE MITTENS
Cuff: With smaller size needles cast on 54 sts. Divide on 3 needles, being careful not to twist sts. Work in k 1, p 1 rib for 2½ ins or until cuff is as long as you wish.

Hand: Change to larger size needles and work in ss for 1 in.

Thumb Gore:
Rnd 1: K 26 sts. Place marker, inc in each of next 2 sts, place second marker. K remaining 26 sts.
Rnd 2: Work even.
Rnd 3: Inc after first marker and before second marker.
Rep Rnds 2 and 3 until there are 18 sts between markers. Work even until mitten reaches angle of thumb and index finger.

Thumb: K to marker. Sl these 26 sts on holder. K thumb sts. Sl remaining 26 sts on second holder.

Divide thumb sts on 3 needles, casting on 2 additional sts (20). Work even in ss until thumb is long enough.

Thumb Decrease:
Rnd 1: K 2 tog around.
Rnd 2: K 2 tog around.
Draw yarn through remaining sts; pull tight and fasten.

Finish Hand: Sl 26 sts from second holder to left needle. Join yarn and k them. Insert yarn marker at end of this needle. Sl 26 sts from remaining holder to 2 needles. K these 2 needles, picking up 1 st from base of thumb at end of last needle. Insert another yarn marker. Pick up another st at base of thumb and continue working on 54 sts which are now divided evenly by the 2 yarn markers. When mitten is 1¾ ins less than desired finished length, begin dec.

Decrease for Tip:
Rnd 1: K 2 tog, k to 2 sts before first marker, k 2 tog. Sl marker, k 2 tog, k to 2 sts before second marker, k 2 tog (4 sts dec).
Rnd 2: Work even.
Rep Rnds 1 and 2 five times more. Weave remaining 30 sts tog.

A little bit of old Mexico...

Aztec Abstract

Beginner

Stitch up a fantasy of ancient times with this masculine design. (Shown on page 46.)

Size: 12 inches.
Yarn: 4 oz Knitting Worsted Weight.
Needles: 1 pair single point in size needed to reach gauge, 1 pair two sizes smaller (for Two Needle Mittens); 1 set double point in size needed to reach gauge, 1 set two sizes smaller (for Four Needle Mittens).
Gauge: 5 stitches (sts) per inch.
Note: Pattern is the same for right and left mittens.

TWO NEEDLE MITTENS

Cuff: With smaller size needles cast on 60 sts. Work in k 1, p 1 rib for 2½ ins or until cuff is as long as you wish. Rest of mitten is worked in ss.

Hand: Change to larger size needles and work even for 1 in. End with p row.

Thumb Gore:
Row 1: K 29 sts, place marker, inc in each of next 2 sts, place second marker. K remaining 29 sts.
Row 2: P.
Row 3: Inc after first marker and before second marker.
Rep rows 2 and 3 until there are 20 sts between markers. Work even until mitten reaches angle of thumb and index finger. End with a p row.

Thumb: K to marker. Sl these 29 sts to holder. K to next marker, cast on 1 st. Sl remaining 29 sts to second holder. P back on thumb sts, cast on 1 more st. Work even on 22 thumb sts until thumb is long enough, ending with p row.

Thumb Decrease:
Row 1: K 2 tog across row.
Row 2: P.
Row 3: K 2 tog across row. End with k 1.

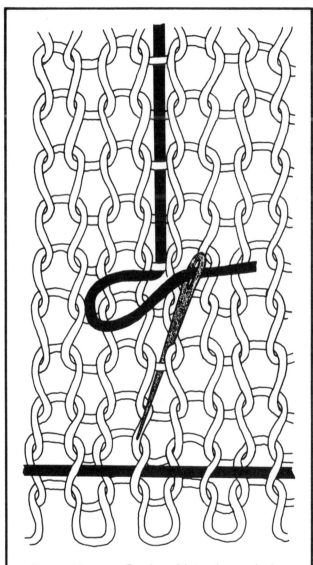

Aztec Abstract Design: Make the vertical lines with a running stitch going over 1 thread and under 1 thread (see drawing). Work the horizontal running stitches with your needle going over 1 thread and under the next.

Draw yarn through remaining sts, pull tight and sew thumb seam.

Finish Hand: Sl 29 sts from first holder to right needle. Join yarn and pick up 2 sts from base of thumb seam, sl 29 sts from second holder to left

CONTINUED ON PAGE 47

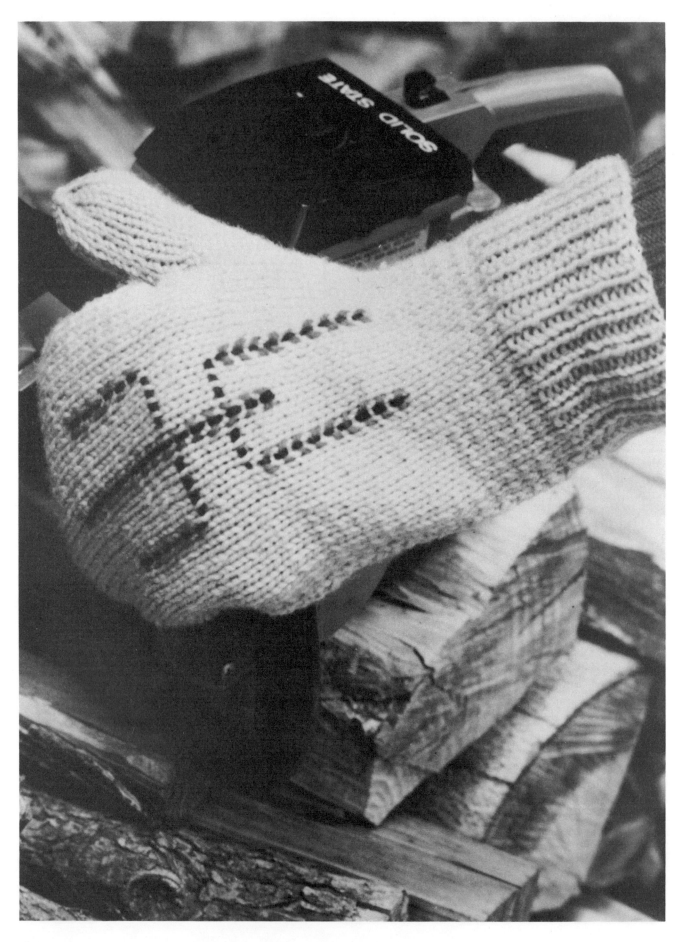

AZTEC ABSTRACT: CONTINUED FROM PAGE 45

needle and k them (60). Continue to work even until mitten is 2 ins less than finished length. End in p row, inserting marker in center of last p row.

Decrease for Tip:
Row 1: K 2 tog, k to 2 sts before marker, k 2 tog, sl marker, k 2 tog, k to last 2 sts, k 2 tog (4 sts dec).
Row 2: P.
Rep these two rows 6 times more. Weave remaining 32 sts tog. Sew side seam of mitten.

FOUR NEEDLE MITTENS

Cuff: With smaller size needles cast on 60 sts. Divide on 3 needles, being careful not to twist sts. Work in k 1, p 1 rib for 2½ ins or until cuff is as long as you wish.

Hand: Change to larger size needles and work in ss for 1 in.

Thumb Gore:
Rnd 1: K 29 sts. Place marker, inc in each of next 2 sts, place second marker. K remaining 29 sts.
Rnd 2: Work even.
Rnd 3: Inc after first marker and before second marker.
Rep Rnds 2 and 3 until there are 20 sts between markers. Work even until mitten reaches angle of thumb and index finger.

Thumb: K to marker. Sl these 29 sts on holder. K thumb sts. Sl remaining 29 sts on second holder. Divide thumb sts on 3 needles, casting on 2 additional sts (22). Work even in ss until thumb is long enough.

Thumb Decrease:
Rnd 1: K 2 tog around.
Rnd 2: K 2 tog around. End with k 1.
Draw yarn through remaining sts; pull tight and fasten.

Finish Hand: Sl 29 sts from second holder to left needle. Join yarn and k them. Insert yarn marker at end of this needle. Sl 29 sts from remaining holder to 2 needles. K these 2 needles, picking up 1 st from base of thumb at end of last needle. Insert another yarn marker. Pick up another st at base of

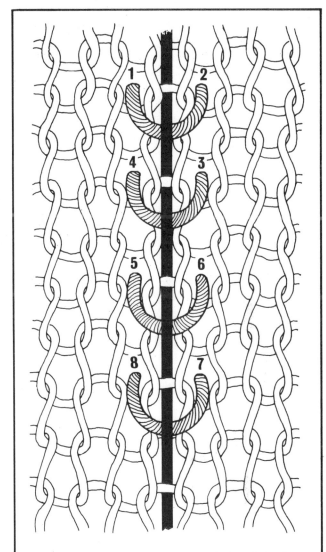

Complete the vertical running stitches by using a contrasting color to work the looped part, beginning on alternate sides. For this, bring the yarn up at 1 under the vertical st, and down at 2 (see illustration).

thumb and continue working on 60 sts which are now divided evenly by the 2 yarn markers. When mitten is 2 ins less than desired finished length, begin dec.

Decrease for Tip:
Rnd 1: K 2 tog, k to 2 sts before first marker, k 2 tog. Sl marker, k 2 tog, k to 2 sts before second marker, k 2 tog (4 sts dec).
Rnd 2: Work even.
Rep Rnds 1 and 2 six times more. Weave remaining 32 sts tog.

ZIG ZAG CHAIN: CONTINUED FROM PAGE 19

Row 3: K 2 tog across row. End with k 1.
Draw yarn through remaining sts, pull tight and sew thumb seam.

Finish Hand: Sl 16 sts from first holder to right needle. Join yarn and pick up 2 sts from base of thumb seam, sl 16 sts from second holder to left needle and k them (34). Continue to work even until mitten is 1 in less than finished length. End in p row, inserting marker in center of last p row.

Decrease for Tip:
Row 1: K 2 tog, k to 2 sts before marker, k 2 tog, sl marker, k 2 tog, k to last 2 sts, k 2 tog (4 sts dec).
Row 2: P.
Rep these two rows 2 times more. Weave remaining 22 sts tog. Sew side seam of mitten.

FOUR NEEDLE MITTENS

Cuff: With smaller size needles cast on 34 sts. Divide on 3 needles, being careful not to twist sts. Work in k 1, p 1 rib for 2 ins or until cuff is as long as you wish.

Hand: Change to larger size needles and work in ss for 1 in.

Thumb Gore:
Rnd 1: K 16 sts. Place marker, inc in each of next 2 sts, place second marker. K remaining 16 sts.

Rnd 2: Work even.
Rnd 3: Inc after first marker and before second marker.
Rep Rnds 2 and 3 until there are 12 sts between markers. Work even until mitten reaches angle of thumb and index finger.

Thumb: K to marker. Sl these 16 sts on holder. K thumb sts. Sl remaining 16 sts on second holder. Divide thumb sts on 3 needles, casting on 2 additional sts (14). Work even in ss until thumb is long enough.

Thumb Decrease: K 2 tog around. Draw yarn through remaining sts; pull tight and fasten.

Finish Hand: Sl sts from second holder to left needle. Join yarn and k them. Insert yarn marker at end of this needle. Sl sts from remaining holder to 2 needles. K these two needles, picking up one st from base of thumb at end of last needle. Insert another yarn marker. Pick up another st at base of thumb and continue working on 34 sts which are now divided evenly by the 2 yarn markers. When mitten is 1 in less than desired finished length, begin dec.

Decrease for Tip:
Rnd 1: K 2 tog, k to 2 sts before first marker, k 2 tog. Sl marker, k 2 tog, k to 2 sts before second marker, k 2 tog (4 sts dec).
Rnd 2: Work even.
Rep Rnds 1 and 2 two times more. Weave remaining 22 sts tog.

RING CABLE FISHERKNIT: CONTINUED FROM PAGE 29

Palm: K 2 tog, k to last 2 sts of Rnd, k 2 tog.
Rnd 2: Work even, maintaining rib pattern on back.
Rep above 2 dec Rnds 4 times more. Weave remaining 28 sts tog.

LEFT MITTEN

K same as right mitten through first 8 Rnds of pattern. To reverse thumb position work Rnd 9 palm sts as follows: K 20, place marker, inc in each of next 2 sts, place marker, k 2. Continue thumb gore to correspond to right mitten.

Thumb: Work Rnd 24 same as Rnd 8 up to last 2 sts of Rnd. K these 2 sts, sl to holder.
Rnd 25: Work 26 back sts as for Rnd 1 and sl these to same holder. K to first marker in palm. Sl these 20 palm sts to second holder. Cast on 1 st, k 18 thumb sts, cast on 1 st. Finish thumb as for right mitten.

Finish (Left) Hand: Sl 26 back sts to left needle. Join yarn and work these 26 sts as in Rnd 2. Sl 20 palm sts to left needle and k, pick up 2 sts from base of thumb and work 2 remaining palm sts from holder (50). Resume 8 Rnd pattern sequence beg with Rnd 3, working even until you have 48 Rnds. Finish as for right mitten.